JESSE CARR MD

Got a Bad Picker?

I0141235

MLN Productions

MLN Productions

ISBN: 978-0-578-15958-4

PRINTED IN THE UNITED STATES OF AMERICA

Contents

Introduction

I've been a psychiatrist for over twenty-three years. In that time I've seen thousands of patients in multiple venues, all ages and conditions. Early in my practice, while working with seniors, I noticed a common theme of regret among some of my female patients--regret about their relationships and the men who caused them so much heartache. This included the men they stayed with through the years, wishing they had left them years ago, as well as missed opportunities during their youth to be with a good man. It was sad to see so many women feeling as if they had wasted their lives and youth on losers.

I subsequently started watching and listening to my younger patients about their relationship choices and consequences. They too complained about relationship dissatisfaction, how badly their men treated them, and how hard it was to find a good guy. It was somewhat surprising that so many nice women were choosing guys that treated them poorly, and often tolerating it for a long time.

There seemed to be some sort of unconscious attraction to and weakness for these losers, despite getting very little out of these relationships. It seemed as if their ability to choose a good partner was malfunctioning or they had a bad picker.

Maybe too much reliance on emotions or feelings went into these decisions. Being more objective has some merit, considering the fact that arranged marriages have about a 4% divorce rate vs. 'Love' marriages at 40-50% divorce rate. Arranged marriages are purely objective-- the family chooses the partner based on similar background, beliefs, culture and socioeconomic status. While I'm not advocating arranged marriages, these statistics suggest that using some objectivity in our dating and marriage picking may be in order.

Sarah is a 32-year-old female who works as a school counselor and has an 11-year-old son. She met her ex-husband, Ralph, when she was a freshman in college. Ralph was her first serious boyfriend and it seemed exciting at first, being in love and full of passion. He was attractive, four years older, charming, a bit of a ladies' man. But early on there were warning signs: Ralph had substance abuse issues, he dropped out of college, then had trouble keeping regular work. She thought she could change him.

Sara got pregnant in her senior year of college, but was able to finish and still support the family. Ralph seemed to take out his frustrations on Sara as he became more and more cruel, negative, and controlling. Despite being quite jealous, Ralph went on to have multiple affairs of his own, along with frequent relapses. Their relationship continued to be a tumultuous cycle of fights, breakups and subsequently make-ups for the sake of the children.

Sara finally ended it after he was caught cheating with one of her co-workers. Sara's subsequent relationship seemed to have a similar pattern and outcome. Sara came to the conclusion that all men are dogs and can't be trusted. Does Sara have bad luck with men or does she have a bad picker? Could she have used some rules to help her with her choices?

In my practice, I encourage the use of the 80/20 rule, which suggests that we work (and choose) smarter to maximize the power of our work/choices. The 80/20 rule was developed by Pareto, an economist who noticed that 80% of the peas in his garden were produced by only 20% of the pods. He also noticed that 80% of the land in his area was owned by only 20% of the landowners. From these and other observations, he developed the Pareto principle or the 80/20 principle used in economics. However, this rule has widespread applications in every walk of life, including the choices we make in relationships. This rule simply describes the relationship between a few root causes (20%) which create most of the results (80%). The trick is to find those few key choices, methods, strategies, and rules that make the most impact.

The quality of our lives seems to hinge on a few key decisions at key points in our life's journey--none more impactful than who we choose as our life partner.

In this book, we will explore potential root causes and consequences of making poor relationship choices. Then, most importantly, how to enhance and fix a bad picker. And lastly, how by becoming your own matchmaker, by using objective data, rules, and strategies you can make the best choices for your happiness. The strategy is to act as if you were matchmaking for your very best friend, but in reality you're gaining self awareness and making more objective and intuitive decisions for yourself.

The case studies used in this book are based on real people, but the names and stories have been modified and/or combined to protect confidentiality.

CHAPTER 1

How do you know if you have a Bad Picker?

"I'm a karate man, I bruise on the inside."
...Billy Ray Valentine played by Eddie Murphy in *Trading Places*

Some of us know we make poor choices in relationships, but can't help ourselves. We seem drawn into them like a moth to a flame. Others have no clue despite convincing evidence to the contrary. It's like the audience watching a horror movie and knowing the characters always make the wrong choices. This, of course, leads to their untimely deaths, but the characters have no awareness.

Some of us just make excuses for our partner's inadequate behavior, like Billy Ray in *Trading Places*. We seek to avoid the cognitive dissonance between who we are and what we envision ourselves or our relationship to be.

If you are not sure whether you have a bad picker, then ask yourself the following questions (if five or more are positive then you probably have a bad picker)

1. Does he mistreat you? Is he disrespectful?

2. Does he cheat on you?

3. Is he immature?

4. Does he think he's a player or wants to be?

5. Is he always looking at other women? Even if you are around?

6. Does he often put you down? Is he negative, critical, or judgmental toward you?

7. Is he cocky, arrogant, only thinking of himself? Does he blame others for his problems?

8. Are you his last priority? Is he selfish?

9. Is he often a no-call, no-show for your dates?

10. Does he often not pay for dates?

11. Is he frequently out of work? Does he have a car?

12. Is he unavailable (emotionally, married, seeing other women)?

13. Is he a liar?

14. Is he abusing substances? Or does he have other addictions?

15. Do you feel you need to change him or can you accept him as he is?

16. Are you the only one who 'understands' him?

17. Do your friends and family like him?

18. Is he violent or does he have a history of violence? Criminal activity?

19. Is he manipulative, coercive, or exploitive? Is he suspicious or controlling?

20. Is he supportive? Does he listen? Does he have empathy?

21. How does he treat the other women in his life? (mother, sister, coworkers)

22. Does he support himself?

23. Does he stay out all night without you? Or refuse to tell you where he has been?

24. Does he not allow you to see his phone?

> "Women must stop complaining about men,
> until they get better taste in men."
> --Bill Maher

If you are in a relationship and unsure if you made the right choice, then it may be helpful to take a relationship survey. Here are two reliable scales:

1. General relationship satisfaction survey from Hendrick S. S.

2. Relationship satisfaction scale from Burns, David D.

General relationships satisfaction survey

	Low				High
1. How well does your partner meet your needs?	1	2	3	4	5
2. In general, how satisfied are you with your relationship?	1	2	3	4	5
3. How good is your relationship compared to most?	1	2	3	4	5
4. How often do you wish you hadn't gotten into this relationship?	1	2	3	4	5
5. To what extent has your relationship met your original expectations?	1	2	3	4	5
6. How much do you love your partner?	1	2	3	4	5
7. How many problems are there in your relationship?	1	2	3	4	5

Scoring
Questions 4-7 are reverse scored.
The higher the score the more satisfied with the relationship.

1. General relationship satisfaction from Hendrick S. S. (1988). A generic measure of relationship satisfaction. Journal of Marriage and the Family, 50, 93-98

	Very Dissatisfied	Moderately Dissatisfied	Somewhat Dissatisfied	Neutral	Somewhat Satisfied	Moderately Satisfied	Very Satisfied	Sub Totals
	0	1	2	3	4	5	6	
1. Communication and openness								
2. Resolving conflicts and arguments								
3. Degree of affection and caring								
4. Intimacy and closeness								
5. Satisfaction with your role in the relationship								
6. Satisfcation with the other person's role in the relationship								
7. Overall satisfaction with the relationship								
Sub Totals								
Total Score								

Scoring Key

Level of Satisfaction	Total Score	M	D				
extremely dissatisfied	0 - 10						
very dissatisfied	11 - 20						
moderately dissatisfied	21 - 25						

Relationship satisfaction scale. From Burns, David D. (1993) Ten days to Self-Esteem. New York, NY: HarperCollins

CHAPTER 2

Causes of Bad Picking

"All the world's a stage, and all the men and women merely players; they have their exits and their entrances."
--William Shakespeare

There are a multitude of forces that contribute to women making poor relationship choices. Some of us are going through the motions, just pretending, playing a character or a role assigned to us by outside forces. We are living life without awareness of who we are or what drives us. So, we date or marry whomever is playing our counterpart in this cosmic play of life.

"The greatest way to live with honor in this world is to be what we pretend to be."
--Socrates

Some causes of poor relationship choices are more biologically-based, others more superficial, and some deeply rooted in our past. The common theme of bad picking seems to be the use of our primitive or reptilian brain over the new brain (neocortex- cerebral hemispheres, responsible for reason, logic, self-awareness).

Our primitive brain acts on instinct and emotions and is automatic in function and typically outside of our awareness. It controls essential processes like breathing, heart rate, digestion, and reproduction. It also has a protective function, including the flight or fight response to signals of danger. We share this primitive or reptilian brain with all reptiles and mammals who are reactive based on instinct.

In this chapter, we will explore a few common reasons of poor picking behavior:

I.   Alpha male syndrome

In the animal world the a-male (alpha male) is the king of the pack, the leader, the strongest, the protector. He takes what he wants because of his reputation as the most dominant (badass). Therefore, he gets his choice of mates and gets to shit, eat and mate first (not necessarily in that order). It's no wonder that from an evolutionary perspective, females would want the strongest male for protection and their genes for future offspring. They are just following the natural law of: survival of the fittest, or mother of the next king or line of kings.

Back in the caveman days, it would make sense for a woman to make a similar choice, picking an a-male for reproductive purposes because he was the most fit to survive and provide for her and her offspring. In those days, the a-male may have been the strongest, but not necessarily the best companion or the wisest. The a-male's top priority was to stay alive and pass on his genes as far and wide as possible. Lifespans were short, secondary to the hostile environment, leaving humans to focus on just the basic needs, as outlined in Maslow's first two hierarchy of needs (i.e., physiological and safety) compared to higher needs, (i.e., love and belonging, esteem needs, self actualization, transcendence).

Fortunately, there are other evolutionary priorities in modern times and some men have evolved beyond just using their primitive brain.

Unfortunately, there are still some of these so-called a-males out there who take risks, have trouble investing in a relationship, remain selfish with a sense of entitlement—as if they deserve multiple partners at the same time (without guilt), and view love as a game to win. He uses all available tactics with the winning goal of spreading his seed to as many females as possible. He's still stuck in the Dark Ages, often unaware of his underlying motivations. Thus he misses out on the higher hierarchical needs of a loving, trusting, and intimate connection to a partner (a more fulfilling relationship).

Some women are unaware of the reasons why they feel drawn to these types of men. They continue to try as they might to change them into suitable companions, often feeling disappointed and concluding that most men are dogs, though, they still try to house train them anyway.

II. Biological drives

Woman are biologically programmed to gravitate toward men with higher testosterone levels. These men tend to be more attractive and dominant. This strong attraction could contribute to errors in selection, especially if you value fidelity, companionship, parenting, or agreeableness.

A problem is that higher testosterone levels are also associated with cheating, needing more novelty in sexual partners, and violence in relationships

Research suggests (reference 1) that males with signals of higher testosterone levels are found to be more attractive to females. These signs include characteristics like a square chin, well- defined brow ridges, bigger noses, muscular physiques, symmetry, and deeper voices (all related to higher testosterone levels). These signs are indicative of dominance or higher status.

Pheromones also play a major role in mate selection. Women find men (again with higher testosterone levels=greater pheromone production) with a more masculine *scent* more attractive, even more so than visual cues.

To illustrate this, a research study asked women, without actually seeing the males, to smell the t-shirts of men. They rated the t-shirts of the more symmetrical men as more attractive.

Symmetry is associated with increased testosterone and increased pheromones production. This effect was even greater during ovulation (which occurs between days 11-21 of the menstrual cycle). Hence, when women are most fertile, they find these males even more irresistible...be careful during ovulation.

Females have more orgasms with more symmetrical mates. This contributes to the strong bonding effect to a mate and aids in conception, i.e., better sex. Also, more symmetrical men (symmetry =attractiveness=higher testosterone levels) produce higher quality sperm (more sperm/ejaculate, faster swimmers) which aids in conception.

There are strong biological drives, often outside of our awareness, to mate with males with higher testosterone levels. This may explain the attraction to, and the reason we continue to go back for more, despite negative experiences.

III. Why do some women love the bad boy?

Women may be attracted to the bad boy secondary to this unconscious evolutionary drive for the alpha male (high testosterone male). They have similar traits, i.e., taking what they want, ruling through intimidation, cockiness, indifference, marching to their own beat, no fear, mysterious, not caring what others think or say (including you), dominance. It may be for similar reasons that some women love the book *50 Shades of Gray* and find it so exciting...a combination of attraction to an a-male embodied in a bad boy.

Human nature suggests that we love what we can't have...the intrigue of unpredictability and desire for what's new. Studies show that our brains' pleasure center lights up more to unpredictability than for sameness—thus, supposedly rewarding us for novelty-seeking. It's like the law of scarcity...the less available the more desirable. These men often seem unavailable emotionally, which ironically makes them more attractive.

The confidence of a bad boy (not giving a shit attitude) can be attractive as hell. It can be a signal of dominance, which is picked up by our primitive brain for reproductive purposes.

Many women unconsciously love the chase/competition of trying to get what other women desire, but can't seemingly have consistently for themselves, making it an ego boost when they do get these males' attention even for a short time. This just reinforces continued bad behavior. The bad boy ride can be a thrill, growing even more enticing if you are bored with your own life.

Others are drawn to the forbidden or what is taboo. It can be very exciting to rebel from convention, especially if you have been a good girl all your life. Ergo, choosing someone who is married, having a secret affair with a bad boy, or rejecting parental ideals for your life i.e., dating outside of your race, culture or socioeconomic class. Some combination of these can explain various poor choices.

We can fall for this illusion of masculinity, i.e., selfishness, being aloof, unavailability, cheating, unreliability, instead of opting for a partner willing to be caring, supportive, intimate and appreciative.

This illusion of masculinity starts at an early age. I noticed some of my 13 y/o daughter's male friends fighting to demonstrate dominance on the playground, all the while watching to see if the females were looking. It seems to work. Even competition at sports are proxies for showing an illusion of masculinity. These behaviors can be false signals of biological fitness.

Men who are viewed as dominant, can arrive there via two divergent pathways, A vs B:

A. Cockiness/boastful (false pride-not true confidence, covering up for deep-seated insecurity) vs.

B. Authentic confidence (positive feelings based on actual accomplishment).

A. Antisocial tactics: coercion, manipulation, aggression with an entitled attitude- poor relationship material vs.

B. Pro-social behaviors: hard working, cooperative, agreeable, with a sincere attitude-good relationship material.

For many of us, this bad boy act wears thin as we mature. We discover that the excitement of the bad boy ride is pretty rocky in the long run. Although, a few of us remain stuck in this cycle, partly because of the bonding effect of passionate orgasms with the release of oxytocin (the love hormone). This can be a powerful force keeping you going back for more despite negative consequences. This bonding effect contributes to poor judgments and choices, almost like you are under the influence of a drug.

Likewise, people who are unfaithful often get a thrill from cheating (the cheater's high) and can become addicted to such behaviors (remember, 30-45% of cheaters cheat again, with even higher rates for bad boys).

Betty, a 41y/o college grad, reports meeting a nice, but shy guy, George, while in college. They became great friends. He was sweet, reliable, and considerate. He had all of the objective qualities you'd look for in a potential mate. They went out a couple of times, but soon got stuck in the friend zone when a bad boy, Mark, showed up.

Mark was exciting and the sex was great. He was fun, adventurous, and had the gift of gab. On the downside, he was unavailable, in that he rarely called, except for a booty call, and often showed up late for dates, if at all. Despite the roller coaster ride of a relationship, Betty continued to be drawn to Mark even when he was simultaneously seeing other women.

She continued to be thrilled and chased the bad boys until she married one of them. Twelve years later, after an unhappy marriage and a messy divorce, she met up with George again. This time around he seemed much more attractive; they married and are happy with three children.

IV. Low self-esteem

The negative selfie stick

My daughter loves taking selfie-pictures of herself with her cell phone. In a gadget magazine, I found this expandable stick to which you can attach your cell phone. Along with a remote it aids in taking pictures of yourself. My family loves it. There is no need to ask someone else to take your pictures while on vacation--everybody is in the picture.

This made me think of the brain's "selfie stick" that records everything, but also has analyzing powers, like our primitive brain, to protect us from danger.

This imaginary selfie stick records everything from our past and present. When it gets enough data it's capable of making inference about us. It then reminds us of the lessons learned throughout our lifetime. This (short cut) organizes relevant data and develops rules to help us make quick decisions and judgments about everything, including others, ourselves and the world.

Once the selfie stick makes a rule, it is very hard to change its mind. For example, if your parents called you "stupid" long enough, the selfie stick concludes this must be true. It then replays these messages, just when needed to remind us of the rules, even if evidence to the contrary exists. Somehow, the selfie stick knows to pay extra special attention when our early caregivers speak or act toward us. It's as if it goes into super slow motion or high definition mode to assist in making rules or self-guiding statements. These self statements often go unchallenged (because they may be outside our awareness), but they can lead to significant hardship and low self-esteem.

Common rules or self statements of girls with low self-esteem include:

"You're no good..."

"You don't deserve better..."

"Nothing good ever lasts..."

"The world is dangerous..."

"It's my fault..."

"He is just being a man..."

"I can change him..."

"Nobody will ever love you..."

"You're unlovable..."

"It's your fault daddy left..."

"It's your fault Mom doesn't care..."

"You're not pretty enough..."

"You're too fat..."

"Life is unfair"...fill in the blank "You're too......................".

After a while you just incorporate these self statements into who you are, unless you challenge them and develop a more balanced view of yourself.

Low self-esteem can lead to poor selection of partners. In addition, we put up with bad behavior because we feel we don't deserve better. We may be unaware of the rules the negative selfie stick has put in place for us, but they operate using the same ploys until we gain self awareness and push the delete button. If we feel unworthy, then we may choose the man we think we deserve, or just the first one that happens by.

Sometimes we try to boost our self-esteem with our choice of mates. If our mate is viewed as desirable by society, then we may feel an enhancement in our self-esteem. i.e., trophy wife, dating or being with a celebrity (the groupie phenomenon), dating a powerful man. This self-esteem-based choice may not be the best companion or may not be well suited for us.

Other times the selfie stick creates a fantasy of a perfect man who will come in and rescue us and our low self-esteem. Somehow, this never seems to happen adequately enough, causing us to unconsciously reject suitable mates, while looking for the fantasy.

Destiny is a 25y/o personal fitness trainer--by all accounts very beautiful. She has been in a cycle of dating bad boys who treat her poorly. They are often unemployed and take her for granted. She keeps trying harder and harder to make these relationships work, but the guys seem to just want and take more from her. Her selfie stick tells her she's not beautiful and should just take what she can get.

It is possible that the negative selfie stick can come to errone-ous conclusions.

V. Poor attachment style

We, as humans, are very adaptive. Even from a early age we learn how to get our needs met. Some strategies are more ef-fective than others, but since we don't choose our caregivers or their response to us, we just have to make the best of it.

Baby Jay, an 18-month-old female, innately knows how to get her needs met. She has an amazing social smile, laugh, and a cute use of a limited vocabulary. She was in my office the other day saying "thank you," "hi," and "mean table" when she bumped her head. Everyone naturally responds to her adorable behavior. She clearly has a secure attachment. She is able to explore and communicate by herself confidently, then returns to her mother for encouragement.

However, if our early caregivers were unavailable, inconsis-tent, neglectful, or unable to meet our needs (despite our best efforts), we may develop an insecure attachment bond. This is about the time the negative selfie stick starts making judgments about ourselves and the world. It often occurs prior to the de-velopment of our verbal memory, which may be the cause of our lack of awareness of our underlying motivations and drives.

Our style of attachment, developed as children, can be life long, with particular consequences for adult relationships. However, it can be modified with insight, awareness and sometimes therapy is needed.

Studies show that about 60% of us have a secure attachment: We grow up feeling safe, secure, and soothed which leads to having more satisfying relationships, more comfort expressing emotions, and better adjustment. We tend to get along better with peers and are often well liked.

20% have an avoidant attachment style: We react with indifference to inadequate caregivers, which leads to mistrust, trouble getting close to others, and problems with intimacy.

20% have an anxious attachment style: We grow up more ambivalent, behaving more frantically and with less confidence, because our needs were inconsistently met. This results in more fearfulness—fear that we won't be loved, suffering from dependence, clinginess and jealousy.

The latter two styles tend to lead to dysfunctional adult relationships, as well as poor choice of partners (Bad picker) because of unmet needs of childhood. By being adaptive, some of us unconsciously try to fill these unmet needs of childhood in our adult relationships. Some just replay maladaptive patterns of the past, i.e., if we feel that our needs won't be met then we choose partners who are consistently unavailable, thus completing a self fulfilling prophecy.

VI. Got Daddy issues?

For women, Daddy issues can be another type of attachment problem of a different stripe. A woman is considered to develop daddy issues when she has a poor relationship or an unavailable/absent father. This spills over into her adult relationships in the form of only dating older men, constantly needing reassurance, engaging in promiscuous behavior (using sex to fill the hole of what's missing), or excessive clinging. These are signs of the classic daddy issues syndrome.

This experience of emptiness or loss often leaves us feeling unloved, guilty, and with a longing for what is missing. We sometimes try to fill these holes by chasing father figures who are unavailable, distant, abusive, or never there.

If we identify with an unavailable father we can unwittingly choose unavailable men or traits of this lost father figure. Sometimes it just feels familiar. Other times we are trying to undo the past by fixing this father proxy in our new relationship, which often turns into failure. We sometimes just replay the past patterns over and over again. The fact that second marriage choices have a 60% failure rate suggests a pattern of inadequate choice of mates, even the second time around.

The consequences of having an absent father are numerous for all of us, according to Edward Kruk Ph.D in *Co-Parenting after Divorce*:

Fatherless children are:

-71% of high school dropouts
-85% of youth in prison
-having earlier sexual experiences
-at greater risk of teenage pregnancy
-90% of runaways
-at increased risk of substance abuse

Until we grieve the loss of the unavailable/absent or abusive father, fix the self esteem hole, and work through the guilt, we may be subject to unsatisfactory relationships secondary to poor choice of mates. This can be continued for generations-your daughter's father leaves because of your poor picker/ issues and then she has the absent father syndrome and it continues... If you lost the love of a father figure, you'll likely look for it someplace else.

Michele is a sweet, mixed-raced female in her early 30s. She works as a manager at a restaurant and is successful at work. Michele was raised without her dad in the picture--a father who had multiple children from different women. She also has three children from different men.

She is always drawn to the same kind of men—those who are unavailable and unwilling to commit to her, including her current boyfriend, Jason. He works as a "hustler" and stays with her at times. Michele often kicks him out due to infidelity. He then goes and stays with his baby's momma. The final straw came when child protective services took her kids away because Jason had drugs in her house. She tried to date some "nice guys" but always felt bored, leading her back to chasing Jason and fighting with his baby's momma for him. Michele often wonders why she is unlucky in love.

This case illustrates poor choices, likely related to daddy issues, attraction to bad boys, and a lack of self awareness--as well as an undoing complex.

VII. You may have an undoing complex.

Wonder why women often choose men like their dads or other father figures? We learn about relationships by watching and mimicking relationships from childhood. It's how we learn most things. For example, a little girl watches her mom get dressed for work—putting on makeup, doing her hair, wearing jewelry. Pretty soon this young girl is playing dress-up, too. She is mimicking her mom's behavior through observation.

The same is true as we watch our parents relate and note how they treat each other, how they fight, make up, their roles, even Mom's choice in mates. If our early home life is disharmonious with acrimony, we may come to believe that is the norm. When older, we may unwittingly recreate in our current relationships the failed dynamics of bad relationships and the disharmonious atmosphere we've witnessed in the past. We try to fix or undo the bad outcome of the past, often with the same results.

Our primitive brain seems to stay fixated on past conflicts and continues to try to fix them by unconsciously recreating the old patterns over and over again. Until your picker gains awareness of old maladaptive patterns, you are doomed to repeat them.

VIII. You get what you give

Putting out negative energy into the universe often causes a return of negativity. It is much like a boomerang. You often get back what you put out. If you are angry, then people often respond in kind. Likewise, if you put out love, kindness, and understanding you are more likely to get it in return. Be careful what you put out there. Just like sharks can sense blood in the water up to a half mile away, we too as humans have an intuitive sense about the energy or aura of others, and respond in kind. This is a function of our old brain. So, even if you don't get what you put out there, at least you will be living in a more harmonious environment.

For example, I'm a swimmer and try to swim every day. If I was to crap in my own pool then I'd just be swimming in crap. However, if I take care of my pool by cleaning and replacing the chemicals, I'll be swimming in a great environment. Likewise, be careful what you put in your pool of life, because you'll be living in it. Similarly, they often say forgiveness is not for the person you forgive, but for yourself, so you don't have to live with all the bitterness, anger, hatred present in your metaphorical pool of life. Therefore, as a consequence of putting out negative energy, we may not be necessarily choosing poor partners, but still attracting and accepting negative partners into our world.

IX. Falling for immature characters based on emotions or superficial traits

The best relationships are based on couples who are equally yoked (similarly matched). Develop the character traits in yourself which you desire in others.

Develop and look for more mature personality character traits (as described in *Feeling Good: The Science of Well-being* by C. Robert Cloninger, M.D., adapted below).

It has been described that our temperaments (mostly from genetics) are managed by our character (mostly from environmental learning). This relationship between the temperaments and character are similar to that of a plane to a pilot. Without the pilot at the controls, the plane might function on autopilot for a while, but eventually would crash and burn.

1. Self-directedness (SD). More mature personality traits of SD include: being responsible, purposeful, resourceful, self-accepting, self-actualizing vs. immature traits of SD: blaming, aimlessness, helplessness, defensiveness, conflicted

2. Cooperativeness (CO). More mature personality traits of CO: tolerant, empathetic, helpful, forgiving, principled. vs immature traits of CO: prejudiced, insensitive, hostile, revengeful, opportunistic.

3. Self-transcendence (ST). More mature personality traits of ST: genuine, self forgetful, holistic/self transpersonal, spiritual, idealistic, contemplative vs. immature trait of ST: conventional, individualistic, skeptical, pragmatic, materialistic

These traits can be measured on the TCI personality test (see reference # 4)

Our primitive brain might not consider a potential mate's character in mate selection. It requires more objective executive function of the new brain, to avoid immature characters (otherwise your relationship is likely to crash and burn).

Mrs. Bailey is a 70y/o female, who has been married for fifty years. She met her husband shortly out of high school. She described him as athletic and admired by all, but quite distant, insensitive, self-centered, and stern. His personality was similar to her emotionally unavailable father. Of course, her mother didn't like him, but Ms. Bailey married him anyway.

She was quite defensive and fearful growing up, because her mom was often on the attack, with constant complaining, put downs, and criticism. She always had a low self esteem, so she jumped at the chance to be with this handsome fireman, despite his lack of caring and concern for her. She thought she could change him, and that she couldn't do any better, even though her girlfriends counseled her to the contrary.

After having two children, her husband grew more and more distant, hostile, and negative. He stopped coming home every night and developed his own life outside of the marriage. He was not very involved in the children's lives either. He probably had an avoidant attachment style as a child.

Now, they are still married, but sleep in separate bedrooms, have had no sex for twenty years, and act only as begrudging roommates. Mrs. Bailey has turned to alcohol to deal with the pain of loneliness, regret and despair. She continues to suffer from a very emotional choice of mate, despite warning signs of an immature character and caution from others.

> "Any fool can criticize, condemn,
> and complain-and most fools do."
> ...Benjamin Franklin

X. Fear of intimacy

Some of us fear openness and are reluctant to accept physical or emotional closeness in relationships. Despite consciously wanting and needing love, as we all do, we feel uncomfortable accepting intimacy.

This can be a source of great difficulty, anxiety, and dismay, because we all need to be:

- loved and cared for/comforted

- understood/validated

- given affection and respect

- shown kindness

- offered companionship and justice

Being in love is actually our natural state. This fear of intimacy is contrary to our natural state and has contributed to difficulties in many relationships. Causes include, repeated early life hurts/traumas, rejection, disappointment, or an insecure attachment. All of these can lead to avoiding painful feelings by avoiding intimacy or closeness for fear of rejection or continued pain. This pattern can continue throughout our lives and affect our sense of self. If we view ourselves as impaired and not deserving of love, we may be reluctant to accept love even when offered and, instead, respond with distancing or anxiety.

This fear of intimacy can contribute to poor choices in mates—picking men who are unavailable physically or emotionally, married men, long distance or internet relationships, immature characters who are incapable of intimacy, abusers of substances, and otherwise.

To avoid closeness, some of us just go through the motions of life, like a robot. We hide behind a mask, pretending connection but all the while protecting our true selves from the world. The negative selfie stick may have concluded that the world is unsafe so people can't be trusted.

The whole world is a stage…so they say. So don't be caught playing a role your entire life. Look behind the mask to know your true self- and to understand your partner as well. Then take off your mask and be your authentic self. It can be quite liberating. It's only in knowing yourself that you can be open to finding and connecting with your life partner.

"There are three extremely hard things: steel, a diamond, and to know one's self."
--Ben Franklin

Florence finally accepted the fact that she was gay at the age of forty-five. She had been going through the motions of life, living by other's expectations. She had been hiding behind a mask for years. After surviving an abusive childhood she developed a fear of intimacy. She was married with children, but living a lie. Her despair became overwhelming and she made a suicide attempt. While on the road to recovery and self awareness, she discovered that she had always been gay, but was in denial all these years. She felt a great weight had been lifted and felt liberated to be true to herself.

Knowing one's self or becoming self aware is the start to making good decisions for our own happiness.

"The unexamined life is not worth living."
--Socrates

CHAPTER **3**

Consequences of having a Bad Picker

"This is your wake-up call...time to go to work."
--movie *Wall Street* by Oliver Stone

In this chapter, we will compare and contrast some of the benefits of a healthy relationship vs. the consequences of an unhealthy partnership.

We talked about some of the consequences of using just the emotional part of our brain to make relationship choices. We tend to end up with the bad boys, alpha males, immature characters, daddy figures, and mates with excessive emotional baggage--most of which leads to chronic disappointment, dissatisfaction, and missed love and intimacy.

In addition, unhappy marriages and relationships can take a toll on our health. Studies have shown that marital stress put women at higher risk for hypertension, abdominal obesity, depression, elevated cholesterol, diabetes, decreased immune function, and increased secretion of stress hormones. (Not to mention the emotional distress and decreased work performance).

This is in contrast to the usual benefits of marriage and healthy committed relationships which confer greater longevity, better health, and wealth.

Freda and Harry have been dating for three years, living together for two. Freda suffers from depression, which seems to be exacerbated by constant conflict and fighting that usually ends up in the police being called.

Harry is a real estate agent but has been out of work since the housing crash. He takes out his frustration on Freda, but she responds in kind. Harry entered the relationship with anger issues, insecurity, and other emotional baggage from childhood. His previous relationships ended secondary to excessive jealousy and domestic violence. Freda thought he had changed.

At work she is distracted and often tearful, ruminating over the most recent fight or getting advice from coworkers. She has been written up twice in the last month and threatened to walk off the job, despite being the only breadwinner in the family. This is a good example of how relationship stress can be overwhelming and cause difficulties at work and home.

The key to any great relationship is to find a partner who is caring and trustworthy with the capacity for intimacy. However, when we open ourselves up to intimacy but are rejected either actively or passively, it can erode our confidence, self worth, and ability to trust. Choosing a mate too immature to be available and participate fully can be devastating.

Angela and Jack were happily married for over eighty years. He was a dentist and Angela was his assistant. On their 80th anniversary, they were asked about the secret of their success. They both said to always put the other one's needs above your own. In the last year of their lives together they were still in love, holding hands as they watched TV together. They died two weeks apart at 102y/o and 100y/o.

> "Marriage is the most natural state of man, and...
> the state in which you will find solid happiness."
> --Benjamin Franklin

I believe the secret to happiness starts with self awareness (know thyself), then finding purpose (know your role), love (commitment to family), hope (something bigger than yourself/ the spiritual, and something to look forward to) and contentment (savoring the moment/gratitude). This is similar to the process of relationship satisfaction. It starts with understanding/empathy for your partner, then growing together with purpose and support, sharing love and hope for the future together, and lastly being content with what you have.

> "He is richest who is content with the least,
> for content is the wealth of nature."
> --Socrates

In contrast, trying to survive a toxic relationship can seriously impair our well-being. It's easy to miss the warning signs or be in denial of toxic individuals we are seeing or planning to see. It's easy to play "the role" while dating for a while, but the masks we hide behind are only temporary. Cracks of our true selves can be seen if aware.

Be leery of overly controlling, insecure, or jealous men because it often leads to emotional and/or physical abuse. Be on guard for men with too much emotional baggage or who are too negative, because it can drain you of your optimism and hope. Deceitful, manipulative, and narcissistic mates are too self-centered to participate in a loving relationship and can get in the way of a healthy partnership and your happiness.

Diane and Jim were dating in high school in a very small town in Iowa. Jim's family essentially owned the town. Being wealthy bankers, they spoiled Jim rotten. He was good-looking, cocky, boastful, but without apparent accomplishments of his own. He used his status to bully and put others down (illusion of masculinity or dominance). Diane's parents loved Jim and encouraged the relationship, thinking it would boost the family's esteem in the community, unaware that he was a bully.

Jim thought he owned Diane with his controlling, possessive, and jealous behavior. Diane was smart, well-liked, and a good girl who wanted to please her parents. She put up with his bad boy behaviors until Johnny came to town.

Johnny was a cool, confident, James Dean type--who got in a little trouble cutting class at times, womanizing, and drinking.

He was never a bully, was always kind, stood up for the little guy, and treated Diane with respect. He listened and valued Diane's opinion.

Diane felt smothered playing the role given to her by her parents and society. She made a choice to take off the mask (the cover that comes with the role) and be true to herself. Diane decided to leave town (and Jim) with Johnny and make a life of her own. She ended up graduating from college with Johnny's support, and now they have a beautiful family. Diane has a career as a college professor and a great relationship.

Life is too short to tolerate such inconsiderate and just plain rude individuals. As I say to my clients all the time—life is not a dress rehearsal while you wait for something better to magically happen, as you just go through the motions of life. Your life is the show; hence, take advantage of every opportunity for happiness.

In this book, I refer to your choices and the consequences of those choices, not to blame you for negative circumstances, but to empower you to take control and responsibility for your own life, because it's the only one you're going to have.

Otherwise, you'll wake up some day feeling like a victim of circumstance, with regret over the life you could have lived but didn't. This can be your wake-up call...time to go to work.

CHAPTER 4

How to Fix a Bad Picker

"Know thyself."
--Ancient Greek maxim written on the forecourt
of the temple of Apollo

"Live in the now."
--Wayne's World

If you are dissatisfied with your relationship choices, the first step to improving your picker starts with working on yourself, and developing your own life and goals. If we enhance ourselves we will be putting out a different energy/vibe and attract something different from the universe. Getting to know yourself better is the key: to understand your patterns, wants, needs, desires, and motivations (self-awareness). Only in knowing yourself can you figure out what you want in others. We must open the door of our minds to new possibilities.

In this chapter, we will explore strategies/tools to enhance self-awareness, self-esteem, care for ourselves and our ability to connect to others.

I. Journaling

Keeping a journal can be a great tool for self-exploration, identifying patterns, reflecting, clarifying, processing, and working through grief and loss. Don't worry about spelling or grammar; just get started because this journal is just for you.

1. Start with writing whatever comes to mind to gain greater awareness of thoughts (free associate for fifteen minutes/day). Then spend a week or as much time as needed to explore items 2-5.

2. Write about your childhood--highs and lows. What were both parents like, their personality traits, how they got along, resolved conflict? Was there infidelity? Communication styles in the household? And how did they treat you? Include siblings, and other important individuals in your life.

3. Write about your greatest strengths and weaknesses. List your talents.

4. Write about past romantic relationships, what happened, your ex-partners' personality traits, and what attracted you to them. Was there intimacy? Infidelity? Did you learn anything about yourself for future relationships. Are you over your ex?

5. Review the journal entries to search for similarities of personality traits in relationships, parents, or other significant people in your life. Do you want your relationship to resemble your parents' relationship? Do you have another ideal relationship model or example? Look for patterns or common themes. Awareness will help with future choices. Consider breaking patterns and trying something new or at the least, make better choices with your eyes opened. All this data can be useful in self-enhancement therapy or coaching.

6. Cognitive Behavioral Therapy (CBT) is a therapy designed to help people identify automatic negative thoughts/self statements. Then it helps replace them with more balanced, accurate thinking. A common CBT technique is to catch it, check it, change it. CBT can help counter the "negative selfie stick" conclusions.

Tara is a 29 y/o professional woman. She has a successful career as a prosecutor and is living life to the fullest except when it comes to love. She dates frequently, but long term relationships seem to escape her.

In therapy, she used journaling to identify a pattern in her relationships. They usually start out well with lots of emotions and passion, but always end in her partners becoming judgmental and critical. This is similar to her relationship with her mother, who was always critical and dismissive. She was trapped in an undoing complex. With awareness, she was able to look for a partner who was more mature, capable of intimacy, and accepting of her as is.

II. Mindfulness Meditation

Mindfulness is a great tool to develop greater self-awareness, stress reduction, self-acceptance, and learning to stay in the moment ("live in the now"). Researcher, Matt Killingsworth, found that we are most happy when we stay in the moment (Reference #19). Other research also supports the use of mindfulness for improving self-knowledge and overcoming barriers to understanding ourselves. (Erika Carlson from Washington University in St. Louis. Reference #20)

It has been said that mindfulness meditation can help bridge the gap between the new brain and the primitive brain--that is, connecting thoughts and feelings, as well as mind and body.

During a crisis or perceived crisis, the emotional brain automatically takes over to protect us, but it also blocks input from the thoughtful new brain. You've heard the term blind rage. This is an extreme example of the automatic functions of the primitive brain.

Therefore, any techniques that keep the rational/thoughtful brain active and connected can be quite powerful.

Mindfulness meditation is...

Paying attention on purpose in the present moment without judgment

Imagine that you are a ship's captain setting sail for the new world for the first time. As you set off on your adventure you keep a journal (paying attention on purpose), noting every new sight and sound as the adventure unfolds (in the present moment). Both good and bad experiences are important and to be learned from. All these experiences add to the excitement, awe, and wonder of being an explorer (we record all experience without premature judgment). Just like a scientific explorer conducting an experiment we objectively collect the data.

Likewise, with mindfulness meditation we experience our thoughts like an observer, with wonder, curiosity and without judgment. Try to observe your thoughts like they are clouds in the sky. Take notice, then let them float by. By observing your thoughts in this way, they can become less powerful and overwhelming. Thoughts are just thoughts and only have the power we have learned to give them.

Be kind to yourself and your thoughts. As your thoughts start to wander or become negative, gently bring focus back to the present moment or the breath. Label them as thinking and gently bring your thoughts back to the breath, like a feather to a balloon. It has been said that our thoughts are like a wild monkey jumping around all over the place. The goal of mindfulness practice is to gently bring the thoughts back to the breath/present as often as it wanders, without judgment.

Use all senses in this practice. When we are mindful, we experience life as it happens. We taste our food more fully and experience sights, sounds, and smells more intensely. We touch and feel more deeply. We become more aware of our thoughts and gain greater awareness of ourselves. We get in touch with our motivations, drives, desires, and needs.

Practice exercise #1 body scan

Get into a comfortable seated position. Place both feet firmly on the floor. Close your eyes. Become aware of your breath as it flows in and out, nice and easy. Notice the natural relaxation that occurs as you breathe out. You are a natural, because you have been breathing all your life. Notice your chest/stomach go up and down as you inhale and exhale (in your mind's eye). Continue to focus on your breath for a few minutes...then imagine your feet set firmly on the floor. Imagine that you can see your feet. Try to breathe a cool relaxing breath into that foot region. Then returning to focus on the breath, imagine you can see the air traveling all the way through the mouth, down the throat, and into your lungs.

Next, imagine your legs....then your abdominal area....then your chest....then your neck....then your head. Try to imagine each region with as much detail as you can for two to three minutes, then return to your breath between each region. If your mind starts to wander, that is normal, just gently bring your thoughts back to your breath. Then resume the body scan. The process of bringing your thoughts back to the present is a valuable brain training exercise that can improve your focus and ability to stay in the moment.

Practice exercise #2. Savoring

Use all five senses to experience a raspberry. Place the raspberry in your hand, feel the texture, then observe the color, shapes, and contours. Smell it carefully. Place the raspberry in your mouth and taste it fully; chew slowly. Remember to breathe.

Try to stay in the moment frequently throughout the day by savoring and experiencing the simple joys life has to offer. Try to use all five senses if possible. Return to the breath frequently between each sense and, as the mind wanders, gently return to the breath and then the other senses. It takes practice. Next, label the thoughts as your mind wanders as "Thinking," without judgment then return to the breath and the senses. Start with five minutes per day and also supplement when stressed. After a while you'll begin to experience life more fully as you live it with existential acceptance.

Research suggests that mindful eating can help re-establish the mind/gut connection. Mindful eating involves eating slower without distraction (like TV, working, reading), savoring each bite, staying present while eating using all five senses, without guilt/judgment, with compassion for ourselves. This leads to healthier choices and to weight loss. When we eat mindfully we choose and eat just what we need.

A 2004 University of North Carolina study of "relative happy, non-distressed couples" showed that couples who practiced mindfulness saw improvements to their "relationship happiness...closeness, and acceptance of one another." In addition, they experienced healthier levels of "relationship stress, stress coping efficacy, and overall stress." (Reference #18)

A mindfulness approach to relationships can also assist with a more peaceful, harmonious life by maintaining the mind/heart connection within yourself and with your partner:

Practice exercise #3 Mindfulness approach to relationships

- Paying attention, on purpose, in the present moment to your partner suggests that they are important to us. Your attention is a very powerful tool to demonstrate your love for your partner.

Connect with your partner frequently by spending quality time without distraction. At least fifteen minutes twice daily, morning and evening, are probably most practical, in addition to sex time. This is a good time for a couple to slow down and get in sync or re-establish the rhythm of the relationship.

Pay close attention by actively listening and responding. Truly share in the joys and happy moments of each other. Replay happy days together to remind each other of why you're together in the first place.

Use all five senses to connect and savor your partner. Take your time looking, listening, smelling, touching, and hugging, in the present moment. Remember to breathe and if your mind starts to wander, bring it back gently. Be gentle with each other and experience your partner without judgment.

Practice exercise #4 Mindfulness approach to relationship communications

- Maintain a 6/1 ratio of positive comments vs. negative criticisms (by both parties, all the time)

- Practice regular acts of kindness

- Practice thankfulness/gratitude and empathy (this helps to avoid complacency and taking each other for granted). Say "thank you," "I love you," and give praise and encouragement frequently throughout the week.

- Engage in peak experiences with your partner. The bonding effects can be incredible. Maslow describes peak experiences as "rare, exciting, oceanic, deeply moving, exhilarating, elevating experiences that generate an advance form of perceiving reality, and are even mystical and magical in their effect on an experimenter."

- Practice best relationship selves exercise (early in the relationship to explore expectations). It's just like the best selves exercise (reviewed later in this chapter), but applied to the relationship.

This exercise helps with exploring what you both really desire, then set goals and a game plan to get what you both want. Each partner should complete the exercise alone. Then compare notes and compromise on a strategy, to accomplish agreed upon goals.

Take 20-30 minutes to write out what you expect from your relationship and the best possible outcome for yourselves as a couple, now and in one, five, and ten years from now. Visualize a future for yourselves in which everything has turned out the way you've wanted it to. You've tried your best, worked hard, and achieved all your goals.

Continue these writing sessions over the next four weeks or as often as you like.

III. Temperament and Character Inventory (TCI) developed by Dr. Cloninger at Washington University in St. Louis, Center for Well-Being. The TCI is an amazing tool that can help us understand ourselves better. Dr. Cloninger answers the following question best, on their website and in the book *Feeling Good: the Science of Well-Being*.

"What is the Temperament and Character Inventory?"

"The Temperament and Character Inventory (TCI) is a set of tests designed to identify the intensity of and relationships between the seven basic personality dimensions of Temperament and Character, which interact to create the unique personality of an individual.

Temperament refers to the automatic emotional responses to experience and is moderately heritable (i.e. genetic, biological) and stable throughout life. The four measured Temperament dimensions are Novelty Seeking (NS), Harm Avoidance (HA), Reward Dependence (RD), and Persistence (PS).

Character refers to self-concepts and individual differences in goals and values, which influence voluntary choices, intentions, and the meaning and salience of what is experienced in life. Differences in character are moderately influenced by socio-cultural learning and mature in progressive steps throughout life. Character takes into account the psychology of the development of personality. The three measured Character dimensions are Self-Directedness (SD), Cooperativeness (CO), and Self-Transcendence (ST).

Each of these aspects of personality interacts with the other one to adapt to life experiences and influence susceptibility to emotional and behavioral disorders. The integration of character and temperament, which reflects the psychobiology of personality, moves this test into a new dimension of understanding ourselves and humanity. This test preserves the time tested and proven aspects of previous psychological and psychiatric data, but negates the charged battles between biology and psychology to form a new integrative whole.

This integration also includes a transpersonal sphere that allows an understanding of how much a person experiences life as an integral part of the universe. The resulting insight helps us to establish a definition and a way to measure an individual's experience of well-being and happiness. With this, we can make a clearer choice of what the best therapy is to help bring someone to a state of happiness and well-being."

Personality tests may also help us in our quest for self-awareness and understanding. I recently was certified to administer the TCI and met Dr. Cloninger in an inspirational seminar which chronicled his thirty years of development and ground breaking research in personality. The energy and excitement in this conference was truly amazing. It felt as if we were on the cutting edge of discovery and understanding of the human personality.

This was truly a peak experience for me. My TCI results and training helped me to re-discover my purpose: to help others in their journey to finding love, peace, (soul) joy, and their role in this life. That why I'm writing this book...just like Don

Cornelius, the host of Soul Train's motto..."until next time I'm wishing you love, peace and soooooooul."

If interested in taking the TCI, contact me at gottabadpicker@ yahoo.com

"Examining our life reveals patterns of behavior. Deeper contemplation yields understanding of the subconscious programming, the powerful mental software that runs our life. Unless we become aware of these patterns, much of our life is unconscious repetition."
--Robert Gerson, a psychotherapist

What about self-esteem?

If we learn to accept, value, and love ourselves, it can create a snowball effect of improving confidence (Self-confidence is a very appealing trait, and draws others to us) and taking better care of ourselves. This includes making good decisions and protecting and putting ourselves in the best position for happiness. This all flows from self-esteem. Some tools to enhance our self-esteem are:

1.   The magnificent you

When I first traveled to Hawaii many years ago, I noticed a crowd of people gathered on the beach looking at something. I thought something had happened, so I asked a guy, "What's going on? What are you all looking at?" He pointed to the sky. I had missed the most beautiful sunset in the world with an amazing collage of colors-red, orange, blue, and yellow as the ocean met the horizon. This experience was just spectacular. I felt swept away in the moment as if I was connected and plugged in with everything. No picture or painting could ever capture that moment. This was definitely an unexpected peak experience.

Each ensuing evening I tried to catch the sunset. No one ever complained about the imperfections of the sunset or that each subsequent sunset was different. The uniqueness or imperfections only enhanced their beauty. Similarly, all of us humans are magnificent and our imperfections, uniquenesses, and variety only enhances our beauty.

We are all wonderful creations. We have the ability to process energy, to sustain ourselves far superior to the most expensive Rolls or Porsche. We are able to adapt, self-repair, and fight off infection better than any army and out-process the most sophisticated computer. Our brains are able to record all sights, sounds, smells, and emotions for a lifetime, better than any camera or smart phone ever created. We have the ability to create, build, and organize like no other animal on earth. We all have the ability to think about thinking and can love and experience love like a gift from our creator. What price would you put on a human being? Priceless!!

What would you pay for a machine that could do all those things? Would it matter if it was getting old or was out of shape? Or if it needed a new paint job or some sort of repair? Would it not still be valuable like an antique? Would the Crown Jewels be any less valuable just because they were old, tarnished or out of style? Likewise, all humans have immeasurable inherent value, which does not change despite flaws, shortcomings, or disease states such as depression or anxiety. We should treat ourselves and others like precious gifts, as if we owned the famous painting "Mona Lisa." We would protect it, be proud of it, treat it like a treasure.

"I don't trust people who don't love themselves and tell me, 'I love you.' ... There is an African saying which is: Be careful when a naked person offers you a shirt."
...Maya Angelou

2. Your best possible selves exercise (adapted from *The How of Happiness* by Sonja Lyubomirsky)

This exercise helps with exploring what you really desire, then helps you set goals and a game plan to get what you want.

Take 20-30 minutes to write out what you expect from your life and what you wish your best possible self to be like now and in one, five, and ten years from now. Visualize a future for yourself in which everything has turned out the way you've wanted it to. You've tried your best, worked hard, and achieved all your goals.

Continue these writing sessions over the next four weeks or as often as you like.

3. Practicing Acts of Kindness

Practicing acts of kindness can enhance our self-esteem by paradoxically focusing on others and developing positive character traits of altruism. The positive energy generated can be quite rewarding and can help us get out of our own heads for a while.

Studies using imaging techniques like a PET scan show that special areas of the brain light up and are reinforced with dopamine release in our pleasure centers when we act in altruistic ways. This only occurs in humans with the development of the neo-cortex (new brain) frontal lobes specifically, which are also responsible for executive functions.

Perform five new acts of kindness per week (but all five in the same day-seems to be more effective if done in the same day) over the next six weeks. Keep a record of these acts and outcomes.

4. Gratitude Journal

Keeping a gratitude journal is a positive psychology technique to assist with self awareness, learning to savor, and fostering contentment.

Oprah is a great advocate of this exercise, and it works well with mindfulness meditation. The following instructions are from a research study given to each participant (Adapted from *The How of Happiness* by Sonja Lyubomirsky)

Studies show an enhancement of positive feelings and life satisfaction with keeping this journal.

"There are many things in our lives, both large and small, that we might be grateful for. Think back over the events of the past week and write down up to five things that happened for which you are grateful or thankful."

For the next six weeks keep a gratitude journal on Sunday, listing five new things starting with the statement..."this week I'm grateful for..."

5. Assertiveness Training

Assertiveness is the ability to protect and assert our legitimate rights to: speak up for oneself, set boundaries and limits on other's behaviors, say "no" without feeling guilty, communicate truthfully and directly without fear--all without violating the rights of others. It also includes the right to live your life as you choose and be responsible for those choices.

"If I am not for myself, who will be for me? But if I am only for myself, what am I? And if not now, when?"
...Hillel the Elder

Being more assertive can enhance our self esteem. Likewise, if we recognize our value then we are more likely to stand up for ourselves. Assertiveness is a skill that can be learned. In contrast to aggressiveness, or passive communication styles often come naturally from our backgrounds or a belief that other's needs, rights or opinions are more important than our own.

Learning to communicate and behaving more directly and honestly can improve: our relationships, decision-making ability, confidence, and our sense of control over our environment.

It can be helpful to be assertive with ourselves as well--by assertively challenging old, out-of-date, self statements that often hold us back. We must recognize when the rules have changed and no longer apply.

For example, when in a war zone, it may be adaptive to be jumpy or on edge...like diving to the floor when we hear a sudden noise (like gunfire in a war zone) but if we dive under a table at dinner, when a car backfires, that's probably no longer helpful. Likewise, our old self statements ("you are not good enough," "your feelings are unimportant," "if you stand up for yourself, then you're just selfish or you won't be acceptable," "go along to get along") may have been an accommodation to developmental demands. Now, however, these statements may just be inaccurate and self-defeating. Therefore, part of being assertive is standing up for ourselves and using relevant strategies in the here and now.

A excellent book on assertiveness training is: *How to be an assertive (Not aggressive woman) woman,* By Jean Bear.

6. Therapy

Therapy can help with self-understanding and self-esteem issues. It can help us work through grief and loss (unmet needs of childhood and self blame), as well as teaching us how to maintain a relationship, especially if we had inadequate role modeling. If you have never seen it, how are you supposed to know how to act and what to do once you pick a good man?

Role modeling is essential for any new endeavor. Seek out someone who has succeeded at whatever you are interested in and inquire as to how they accomplished their goal. Ask them to mentor you. Having a mentor can cut down on the learning curve. In medical school, our rule for learning a procedure was: see one, do one, teach one. I think we all could use a relationship or parenting mentor.

Sometimes therapy can serve as a mentorship. Group therapy, in particular, can be a very efficacious intervention to try out new roles and strategies and get immediate feedback from peers. It's an opportunity to check things out directly instead of just going with assumptions and negative self-statements. It allows an opportunity to practice assertiveness skills, as well as observing how others resolve conflicts, bond and relate to each other. I tell my clients all the time that the group is the perfect testing ground to practice new behaviors in a safe environment. With practice, skills improve as well as confidence and self-esteem.

Therapy can help us work through self defeating patterns from childhood and getting out of our own way to happiness. Understanding the root of self-sabotage can be the start of healing and making good choices in our own best interest.

"We have met the enemy and he is us"
--Walt Kelly

If interested in therapy, you must approach it with an open mind, willing to look at things differently, challenging old ideas and beliefs. Then, find the right therapist (or group) who you can relate to and has the orientation to help you accomplish your goals, i.e., CBT, interpersonal psychothera-py, mindfulness meditation, psychodynamic psychotherapy, group therapy, personality testing like the TCI. It's ok to inter-view several therapists to see if they are the right fit and are equipped to help you with your self exploration/issues.

"Your job is not to figure out how it's going to happen for you, but to open the door in your head, and when the door opens in real life, just walk through it."

--Jim Carey

CHAPTER **5**

Wellness Exercises to Enhance your Picker

"Nothing will work unless you do."
--Maya Angelou

"Just do it."
--Nike slogan

As the medical director of outpatient therapy programs for over twenty years, I've collected a library of coping and self-help strategies. I encouraged the practice of these positive psychology techniques with great success (Best practices in the field- see references in the back). Enhancing your picker just means to optimize yourself, which will vicariously improve your choice in mates.

Here are the top thirty-five best practices. Try them all, then use the ones which work best for you. Sometimes you just have to do it...or just fake it till you make it. Anything worthwhile takes time, focus, consistency and practice. Henceforth, patience is required to appreciate the positive benefits.

Thirty-five tips to promote your well-being:

1. Exercise every day

2. Drink at least eight glasses of water each day

3. Eat plenty of fruits and vegetables at each meal

4. Nurture healthy relationships- spend quality time, pay attention, active/constructive listening, assertive communication, truly share in the joy and happy moments of each other, be loyal, tolerant, maintain confidence, always greet your partner with a smile, a hug and a kiss, be kind and respectful, show gratitude often—say "thank you," enjoy frequent sexual activity, seek out and engage in new (as well as peak) experiences with your partner, 6/1 ratio of positive vs. negative comments to your partner is essential.

For example, if you made a negative criticism of your partner, then your next six comments must be positive. When both partners participate you'll see a more positive relationship.

Use "I", "WE" and "US" statement instead of "you" statements when trying to resolve conflicts (see reference #21)

5. Limit/eliminate or improve unhealthy relationships

The negative energy is not worth the effort

> "I stay away from negative relationships.
> They are energy sapping vampires..."
> --Preity Zinta

6. Learn and practice mindfulness meditation fifteen to thirty minutes/day.

7. Gratitude visit exercise- write a letter of thanks to someone who you have not properly thanked or who has made an impact in your life. Then make an appointment to read the letter to this person and express thanks directly.

> "Practice an attitude of gratitude."
> --common AA saying

8. Best possible selves exercises (see chapter 4)

9. Nurture spiritual/religious exploration

The ability to transcend and connect with the universe or a higher power is a uniquely human ability/characteristic of our new brain. Utilize this ability to the fullest and you won't be disappointed.

10. Practice forgiveness of self and others. Let go of anger and resentment

The ability to forgive and let go of resentment, revenge, anger, and bitterness can actually benefit the forgiver more than the forgiven. Shifting to a more generous, compassionate mindset can reduce stress by decreasing the release of stress hormones. Studies suggest that if we are able to forgive we tend to live longer.

11. Practice smiling and hugging.

Hugging makes you happier. Couples who hug more are more likely to stay together. Hugs tend to release oxytocin, the love hormone, and reduce stress.

A study by Strack, et al, showed that participants who were forced to smile by holding a pencil in between their teeth, viewed humorist material as more funny than controls who were not smiling. Hence, smiling can also have a positive effect on mood and your appreciation of positive events. It can also induce a more favorable response from others to your smiling face.

There seems to be a mind-body feedback loop between the facial muscles and the brain that has a significant effect on mood. Tony Bennett was onto something when he wrote the song "Put on a Happy Face."

"Let us always meet each other with a smile,
cause a smile is the beginnings of love."
--Mother Teresa

12. Savoring exercise- use all the senses; replay happy days

Once a day, try to savor or truly enjoy something you usually rush through i.e., eating, taking a bath, walking, exercising. Then write about the experience, what was different and how you felt using all five senses. Then replay these positive experiences every week.

13. Practice acts of kindness at least one to three times/week, but all in one day. Then write about the experience in your journal. Add these experiences to your replay exercise each week.

The University of British Columbia researchers found that doing nice things for people led to a significant increase in people's positive moods. It also led to an increase in relationship satisfaction and a decrease in social avoidance in socially anxious individuals.

This reminds me of a time when, while on vacation with the family, we were stuck in a parking structure in France. The parking meter wouldn't take a credit card or paper currency. We tried for about ten minutes to change $20 US for Euro coins. Finally, this super nice French gentleman paid our toll and wouldn't take our money in return. We were just amazed by this random act of kindness. The positive feelings lasted the entire day and altered our view of the French people.

14. Listen and accept the wisdom of your body

Mindfulness meditation can help you be more in tune to feedback from your body, mind, and soul.

15. Get adequate rest

Studies show that people who get eight hours of sleep live longer.

16. Live in the moment. It is the only moment we have

17. Work on giving up the need for external approval

18. Become aware and honor your feelings. Express feelings of anger and bitterness appropriately...then let them go...

"Holding on to anger is like grasping a hot coal with the intent of throwing it at someone else; while you are the one who gets burned."
--Buddha

"Whatever is begun in anger ends in shame."
--Benjamin Franklin

19. Stay connected to other human beings and accept them as they are. Be patient with your loved ones, allowing them to evolve in their own time.

"He that can have patience can have what he will."
--Benjamin Franklin

20. Don't pollute your body/mind with contaminants

A number of relationship disasters occur while under the influence. It can clearly cloud our judgment. I recommend limiting important decisions about relationships while under the influence of substances or in a dysfunctional mood state (like depression, mania or severe anxiety).

21. Honor your intrinsic need for enjoyment, especially humor

Humor is a mature defense mechanism and can help us cope with stressful periods, in addition to being a great character trait for both women and men.

Try the three-funniest-things-today exercise- write down the three funniest things that you've seen, heard or participated in today, and why it was so funny. Then review and share these moments with others each week.

22. Don't make assumptions

"Find the courage to ask questions and to express what you really want. Communicate with others as clearly as you can to avoid misunderstandings, sadness and drama. "
--Don Miguel Ruiz from *The Four Agreements*

Instead of making assumptions, find out directly what's going on.

23. Don't sweat the small stuff, try to go with the flow when possible

"If there is no solution to the problem then don't waste time worrying about it. If there is a solution to the problem then don't waste time worrying about it."
--Dalai Lama XIV

Remember the 80/20 rule. Most (80%) of your problems are caused by only a small number of (20%) key root issues/causes. Hence, if you spend your time/energy discovering and fixing the big ticket items you will solve most of your problems. Therefore, take action or let it go--either way you'll be much happier in love and life.

24. Leave emotional baggage at the door; work through your issues so they don't work on you and your relationships

25. Don't take things personally

"Nothing others do is because of you. What others say and do is a projection of their own reality, their own dream. When you are immune to the opinions and actions of others, you won't be the victim of needless suffering."
--Don Miguel Ruiz

26. Don't let fear guide your life and keep you from living your dreams, in love and life

"So many of us choose our path out of fear disguised as
practicality...you can fail at what you don't want, so you
might as well take a chance on doing what you love."
-Jim Carey

27. Find your passion. Engage in peak experiences, find your
flow (also known as the 'zone' in positive psychology. Flow
has been described as the mental state of operations in
which a person is performing an activity, is fully immersed
in energized focus, full involvement, and enjoyment in the
process of an activity, where time seems to fly by) while
learning contentment and enjoying the simple pleasures...

"God's gifts puts man's best dreams to shame."
--Elizabeth Barrett Browning

28. Practice relaxation throughout the day

I recommend taking five deep, slow breaths each time the
phone rings at work or after walking through a doorway. This
way you can decompress frequently and stay present more
often. This also reduces the release of stress hormones that
contribute to stress, heighten anxiety, the metabolic syndrome, and a decreased immune response. If you practice
mindfulness meditation, this strategy can help you to return
to that peaceful state as often as you like.

Being able to relax while maintaining performance may
help you achieve and or sustain flow. Yoga is a good

example of a well-planned flow exercise. With the goal to… "achieve a joyous, self-forgetful involvement through concentration, which in turn is made possible through a discipline of the body."

"The best moments of our lives are not passive, receptive, relaxing times…the best moments usually occur when a person's body or mind are stretched to its limit in voluntary effort to accomplish something difficult and worthwhile. Optimal experience is thus something we make happen."
--Mihaly Csikszentmihalyi

29. Live your life today so you won't have regrets tomorrow

30. Three-good-things exercise

Each day for one week, write about three good things that happened that day and why they happened. Then, continue this exercise every week for the next month.

31. Take the Values In Action (VIA) survey to find your signature strengths of character.

You can find this free survey at:
www.viacharacter.org/

32. Use your top five signature strengths in a new way each day.

33. Practice the full life- 1/3 the pleasant life, 1/3 the engaged life, 1/3 the meaningful life (The Seligman model of authentic happiness; reference # 13)

- the pleasant life: maximizing positive emotions while limiting pain and negative emotions. It includes serenity, contentment, satisfaction, pleasure, faith, hope, and optimism.

- the engaged life: the positive use of individual traits, talents and strengths of character to meet challenges... Aristotle called this the "good life" because it leads to more engagement and flow.

- the meaningful life: connection with, and being of service to, something greater than oneself.

34. Practice assertive listening and communicating daily

"The ultimate freedom is the right and power to decide how anybody or anything outside ourselves will affect us."
--Stephen Covey

35. Practice good habits every day. The more you practice, the easier things become, and before you know it, those habits become second nature.

It has been said that it takes 10,000 hours of practice to gain true mastery over something.

We recently took a trip to China and witnessed two of the seventh or eighth wonders of the world. The Great Wall of China, that stretches 4000 miles and took 200 years to build. And the 8000 Terra Cotta Warriors statues also created over two thousand years ago. Built by 3000 artisans it took ten years to build. What spectacular feats!!!

Likewise, to accomplish most things worthwhile, it takes practice, patience, focus, consistency and rhythm.

CHAPTER 6

How to Train your Picker

"And I want the rest of you cowboys to know something,
there's a new sheriff in town."
--Eddie Murphy in *48 Hours*

Let your primitive brain know that someone else is in charge of the picking. Some say the heart wants what the heart wants, but maybe the new brain knows better. The key to training your picker is to use more objectivity. There is still an important role for emotions and intuition in mate selection, but if an over-reliance on those approaches has failed, then maybe it's time for a new relationship sheriff who can maintain the connection between the new and old brains as well as the heart/soul. Consider becoming your own matchmaker, and approach dating as if you were selecting for your best friend.

Here's an alternative strategy to foster more objectivity:

1. Don't invest too much emotional currency until the potential mates are well known. Don't be afraid to gather information from multiple sources (due diligence) because these choices may be the most important in your life. If one person calls your potential partner an ass, it could just be their opinion, but if two or three people call him an ass...then maybe you should check to see if he has a tail.

> "An investment in knowledge pays the best interest."
> --Benjamin Franklin

(I'm sure Ben was talking about knowing yourself as well as your partner)

2. Use a checklist of minimal qualities that you require in a partner, as well as deal-breakers. Then check them off as you date.

3. High on the list of minimal qualities should be: shared values, compatibility, unselfishness, friendship, similar sense of humor.

If you're spiritual he should share your spirituality. If you're educated, adventurous, materialistic so should he. In other words, be equally yoked.

"Opposites attract, but they are not very happy together."
--Dr. Cloninger

4. Choose qualities that are likely to sustain a relationship: generosity, sensitivity, loyalty, humor, cooperation, acceptance, forgiveness, supportiveness, the ability for contentment, positive life outlook, self-sufficiency, communication skills, adaptability, the ability to compromise and tolerance.

Frank and Karen have been happily married for forty-six years. They are missionaries and report the secret to their longevity as a couple is tolerance, communication, and shared passion for their work. They don't sweat the small stuff and talk through the big problems as soon as they arise. Karen says every night they pull the covers up to their chins and resolve things before they go to sleep.

5. Place looks and status low on the list (these can be less enduring qualities).

"Love looks not with the eyes, but with the mind...."
--William Shakespeare

6. If you're drawn to alpha males, look for a-male traits that are truly attraction-worthy—like having confidence, being assertive (not aggressive), not being affected by peer pressure, staying cool in a crisis, not being afraid to take risks, taking charge when needed. These are traits we all can admire and aspire to possess.

7. Go out with all the nice guys. They may have the positive qualities to sustain a relationship and a family for the long term. If you don't give yourself a chance to get to know them, you may be missing out.

Reacting only to the initial illusion of masculinity may not be as adaptive in modern times (where the smartest, most caring, humorous and contentment genes rule the day). That is, compared to the past when the genetic material of the strongest physically with the greatest capacity for reproduction was valued evolutionarily.

8. Take your time getting to know people. There is very little risk in taking your time, especially with sex. People can put up a good front for a while, but after about six months the true personality starts to break through. In addition, it takes time to meet his friends and family to observe how he relates and treats others. You can tell a lot about a person by the company they keep.

"We can take forever, baby, just a minute at a time."
--Tavares

It can also be enlightening to see how he handles adversity. He may seem like a nice guy when things are going well, but when stressed his true character may emerge. Beware of guys with too much emotional baggage. Nothing can drain the energy out of a relationship, and you, like emotional bags unchecked.

"When someone shows you who they are,
believe them the first time."
--Maya Angelou

9. Cast your net out as wide as possible. Don't just consider the usual suspects. Look in atypical places of
common interest (hobbies, sporting events, classes,
lectures, clubs, alumni associations, book clubs, auto
shows, museums, churches, dance classes, dog parks,
charity events, 5k running events, networking events,
mixers, community events, wine tasting tours, single
cruises and tour groups, etc). Think outside of the box.
Don't be afraid to ask a guy out for a drink, or coffee,
to a sports bar or even a sporting event (what guy could
refuse a date to see his favorite team?). Remember, you
must get out there, to cast your net wide...no guts, no
glory.

If you are having trouble approaching men, then consider
telling them that you are a matchmaker to break the ice
(this is not a lie, because you are a matchmaker for yourself). In preparation for this strategy get some business cards
made up and create a list of questions. Then, ask them if
you can interview them. If they seem interesting, confess,
and keep them for yourself. Otherwise, refer them to a girl-
friend. Grow a thick skin, because rejection is just part of the
process; don't take it personally. I tell my male clients with
social anxiety that dating is a numbers game...expect a 10/1
ratio of rejection to acceptances.

"Sometimes you just gotta say, what the F...
and make your move."
--Tom Cruise in *Risky Business*

Anything that tips the supply vs. demand scales in your favor is using the 80/20 rule.

10. Create your own matchmaking network

Consider linking your efforts with other like-minded individuals who are also looking for love, maybe have a bad picker, and want to find a good man. Why not capitalize on the power, reach and potential of this supportive network of matchmakers. Utilize the 80/20 rule to maximize your efforts with the power of the group.

The network should decide on a standard list of questions to ask these relationship candidates. Then go out and collect objective data that could be shared with the group at lunch or dinner bi-weekly. Each member of the group could take turns selecting from the list collected, then the group could provide support, coaching and encouragement.

However, if these dates were unsuccessful, then this just adds to the data pool for the rest. Always seek referrals from satisfied members to expand the network whenever possible. The reach of this network could be incredible and maybe robust enough to even start a business. This is network marketing, for love, at its best.

11. Tell all the guys that you are seeing several other gentlemen and not ready to get serious with anyone just yet (play the field). High demand can be quite alluring, as well as not making yourself too available (scarcity principle). Plus, it gives you options so you don't put all your eggs in one basket too soon. When we have options, we tend to make better choices. In addition, the more you date, you'll likely learn a lot in the process about what you want. You will also be gaining experience in comparing apples to apples, so to speak.

An example of the power of the scarcity principle:

There are approximately 34 million more men than women in China. This was caused by Chairman Mao in 1948. He encouraged all the people to have as many children as possible, for defensive purposes, because China had been attacked and invaded many times in the past. The result was overpopulation and an inability to feed the population. They subsequently, started the one child per family rule. This rule, along with China's preference of having male heirs, led to the overpopulation of males.

Due to the scarcity rule, women dominate in the mate selection process. As a result the Shanghai men are known to shop, cook, clean, and work full time without complaint. Then they hand over their checks to the wife. This phenomenon occurs because of the scarcity of women and the lengths men in China choose to take to find a mate.

12. Remain confident. Confidence is a draw and can increase your demand, while desperation leaves a pheromonal

stink that can be repelling. Just like animals can sense fear, men can sense excessive neediness or a clinger. Don't chase too hard...it creates the natural tendency to run.

13. Keep a score card. Review it with friends, family, and the network before taking it to the next level. Do your parents approve? (in-law issues can sink or help a relationship survive). If you owned a business would you hire him to run it?

Narrow down the list, then date exclusively for a time to get to know the one person. Tell all other suitors you are off the market.

14. Stay positive and optimistic, because our beliefs can often become our reality. Anything that can cause greater effectiveness or efficiency is worthwhile--whether it's the scarcity principle, or just increasing the number of men you meet for consideration.

15. Use the intuitive sense of the primitive brain to look for a partner with a harmonizing rhythm.

Everything in life has a rhythm, including relationships. A successful partnership must be in sync to survive. It's like two people trying to row a boat together or trying to jump a single rope together or a car engine out of tune. If you are out of sync it just won't work, or not well.

Unfortunately, there are few objective measures to guide us in this process. However, if you are open, honest, listening, and in tune with your inner voice you may hear the report from the primitive brain about your rhythm as well as others. It's like paying attention when the hairs on the back of your neck stand up to danger (mindfulness meditation maybe an effective tool to assist you in this process).

"Everything flows out and in; everything has its tides; all things rise and fall; the pendulum-swing manifests in everything; the measure of the swing to the right, is the measure of the swing to the left; rhythm compensates."
-The Kybalion

16. Explore the possibility of connecting on a deeper level with your potential partner. Check to see if you feel a comfort level, to be yourself, to relax, and to stay in your flow, while you're together.

"Everything in the universe has a rhythm, it dances."
--Maya Angelou

Remember, to do your research, take your time, while staying in the moment. Try to expand your horizons, think outside of the box, shop around, use your intuition, find a synchronizing rhythm, and give yourself a chance to experience something new...it may just be what the doctor ordered.

CHAPTER 7

What if your Picker is not Broken?

"You got to know when to hold'em, know when to fold'em...
when to walk away...know when to run..."
--Kenny Rogers

There are times when you've made the best choice using both the new brain and the old emotional brain, weighed the options carefully, and your relationship still goes sideways. It can be constructive to consider potential pitfalls in relationships in your initial selection of a mate.

Typical forks in the road occur when a couple faces stressors, losses, deaths, role transition, and issues of trust. Those challenges can either bring us together or tear us apart. The natural human tendency for complacency or taking each other for granted can be a relationship death sentence. Other common problem areas include loss of passion, issues around money, sex, children, religion and unrealistic expectations.

This is the point where a tough decision needs to be made. It's hard to know if you should try to work things out or call it a day. Sometimes, couples' therapy can help you to decide if you should hold'em or fold'em. You can also clarify if there is anything left to build on or at least to find ways to end it as peacefully as possible. The relationship satisfaction surveys in Chapter 1 can be helpful as well.

Other questions to consider when faced with this tough life-changing decision:

1. Do you enjoy spending time together?

2. Do you share common values and share common interests?

3. Can you forgive and let go? Can trust be re-established? Are you both open enough to work through the issues? Is he fair-minded?

4. Could you live the rest of your life with him without regret?

5. Do you still like him as a person?

6. If you switched places with your best friend, would you advise her to stay?

7. Are you still able to communicate with each other? Can it be re-established?

8. Do you still feel loved? Understood? Can you still laugh together?

9. Are you still having sex? Do you feel satisfied? Any romance left?

10. Are you still in love? Enough love to stay?

This leads to the next question...do you have trouble making decisions? What if you have a bad decider? That's a topic for the next book.

Here is an example of Agnes making the best decision she could with the available data at the beginning and at the end of her relationship:

Sam and Agnes met while in high school, but didn't start dating until Sam returned from his service in the Army. Agnes moved from a rural town in the South to the big city in the 11th grade. It was a bit of a culture shock. In addition, she was still grieving over the death of her father in a union-organizing uprising three years earlier.

She was the oldest of six kids and shouldered a lot of the caretaking responsibilities for her siblings. Agnes was a reserved, religious young lady, sang in the choir, and did fairly well in school. She always had a dream that she would find the perfect guy to take care of her and make all her dreams come true. Sam befriended her right away and made her feel welcome. She was amazed that Sam paid attention to her, considering he was popular and started on the football team.

Sam was a bright, energetic young man from a well-to-do family. He was ambitious and had big plans for the future, despite dealing with a jealous father whom he could never please and who was both physically and emotionally abusive. Sam coped by stuffing his feelings deep inside and survived only on his hope of escaping and making his own way in the future.

In the beginning Sam seemed to be an ideal choice: No one, including Sam, was aware that he was bringing so much emotional baggage with him into the relationship (his negative selfie stick concluded that "I'll never be good enough " and "I am unlovable").

Agnes also suffered from unmet needs of childhood, never really allowed to be a kid. Never able to fill the hole of losing her father. She had unrealistic expectations in a mate that no one could fill.

The relationship marginally survived. They had four children, a house, two cars, and a dog. They outwardly lived the American dream, but inside the relationship they lived a nightmare with loneliness and dissatisfaction.

The relationship took a serious downturn over religious rearing philosophy and financial stressors. When Sam's previously successful business went under, he turned to alcohol and other women for comfort. He eventually took on the role, modeled by his dad, of the abusive husband ("nothing is so bad, a drink won't make it worse"...AA).

Agnes suffered through years of abuse for the sake of the children. Only her strong faith kept her going. Finally, she left him after learning mindfulness meditation in therapy and gaining self-awareness of her value. She decided that she deserved better.

Her negative selfie stick had been telling her that she made a commitment and must stick it out. It said:

"Life is about sacrifice and your needs don't count."

"If you sacrifice and suffer enough, your reward will be in heaven."

"You can't leave your kids fatherless like your dad left you."

The negative selfie stick can be quite harsh and unforgiving.

This case illustrates the complexity of finding the right mate and then trying to make it work. Their problems were multi-factorial- not being on the same page with religious beliefs, the lack of self awareness, dysfunctional ideas, unrealistic expectations, and emotional baggage that contributed to the poor outcome in this relationship.

On the surface there were no clear warning signs at the beginning, but it's clear that if both partners were committed to working through their issues (leaving their bags at the door) before marriage, there would have been a much better chance of success.

> "I did then what I knew how to do.
> Now that I know better, I do better."
> --Maya Angelou

It can be helpful, when looking for a partner, to find one who is open-minded enough to consider therapy when needed, self-exploration, self-improvement, growth together and the coping skills to adapt and make it work during stressful periods. Remember to consider these typical relationship problematic areas in your initial relationship selection process, as well as how your potential partner might respond in those situations.

In conclusion, if we go through life unaware of our motivations, drives, and self statements, then we are likely to make uninformed choices in relationships and in life. Likewise, if we just go through the motions of life, never really engaged or present, we will be missing out on the fascinating experience of this reality. This includes love, the timeless gift that connects us all and makes us human.

In this book, we first checked to see if we had a bad picker. Next, we explored potential causes and consequences of making poor relationship choices. Then, most importantly, we discussed how to fix and train a bad picker by living in the moment, gaining self awareness, and building self esteem, character and confidence. Lastly, we considered adding more objectivity to our picking by becoming our own matchmaker and engaging both the (new) logical brain and the (old) emotional brain to facilitate living a life full of love and companionship, as it was meant to be.

The End

References

1. Wade, T. Joel. The relationship between symmetry and attractiveness, and mating decisions and relevant behavior: a review. Symmetry 2009,1

2. Shoshanna, Brenda. Zen and the art of falling in love

3. Hendrix PhD, Harville. Getting the love you want

4. Cloninger M.D., C. Robert. Feeling good: The science of wellbeing

5. Weismann, Myrna, et al. Clinician's quick guide to interpersonal psychotherapy

6. Zylowsku M.D., Lidia. Mindfulness prescription for ADHD

7. Rubin, Gretchen. The happiness project

8. Williams, Mark, et al. The mindful way through depression

9. Lyubomirsky, Sonja. The how of happiness

10. Seal, Zindel, et al. Mindfulness-based cognitive therapy for depression

11. Kabat-Zinn, Jon. Coming to our senses

12. Shouler PhD, Kenneth. The everything guide to understanding philosophy

13. American Psychiatric Association, DSM-5

14. Burns M.D., David D. Ten days to self-esteem

15. Ruiz, Don Miguel. The mastery of love

16. Ruiz, Don Miguel. The four agreements

17. Seligman, M. et al, Am Psychol 2006

18. Carson, James W., et al. Behavior Therapy 35, 471-494, 2004

19. Killingsworth PhD, Matt. Greater Good. "Does mind wandering make you unhappy", July 16, 2013.

20. Carlson, Margaret. Perspectives on Psychological Sciences: "Overcoming the barriers to self knowledge: Mindfulness as a path to seeing yourself as you really are". March 2013

21. Bear, Jean. "How to be an assertive (Not aggressive woman) woman."